NORTHSTAR

Writing Activity Book

Focus on Reading and Writing

Introductory

Helen S. Solórzano

SERIES EDITORS
Frances Boyd
Carol Numrich

WRITING ACTIVITY BOOKS EDITOR
Helen S. Solórzano

Longman

NorthStar Writing Activity Book, Introductory

Pearson Education, 10 Bank Street, White Plains, NY 10606

Vice president, instructional design: Allen Ascher
Director of development: Penny Laporte
Project manager: Debbie Sistino
Development editor: Stacey Hunter
Vice president, director of design and production: Rhea Banker
Executive managing editor: Linda Moser
Production coordinator: Melissa Leyva
Production editor: Lynn Contrucci
Production manager: Liza Pleva
Director of manufacturing: Patrice Fraccio
Senior manufacturing buyer: Dave Dickey
Cover design: Rhea Banker
Cover illustration: *Variation VI* by W. Kandinsky, Bauhaus Archive/ET Archive,
    London/SuperStock. © 2002 Artists Rights Society (ARS), New York / ADAGP, Paris
Text design adaptation and composition: Rainbow Graphics
Text font: 11/13 Sabon
Illustrations: T. Cataldo

ISBN 0-13-061435-1

Printed in the United States of America
6 7 8 9 10 11 12 13—VHG—10 09 08 07

CONTENTS

INTRODUCTION

The *NorthStar Writing Activity Book* is a companion to *NorthStar: Focus on Reading and Writing* (the Student Book). Building on the themes and content of the Student Book, the *Writing Activity Book* leads students through the writing process with engaging writing assignments. Skills and vocabulary from the Student Book are reviewed and expanded as students draft, revise, and edit their writing.

The *Writing Activity Book* was developed on the principle that the writing process and writing product are equally important. The units bring students step by step through the process of generating ideas, organizing and drafting content, revising their writing, and editing for grammar and mechanics. Students explore different prewriting techniques to find out what works best for them and for their topic. They experience the cyclical nature of writing, in which the writer is constantly evaluating and revising what is on the page. Through peer review exercises, students practice analyzing and responding to writing in a way that will help them better analyze their own. At the same time, they learn about the structural and rhetorical features of writing. They explore different ways to convey their ideas clearly depending on the purpose and audience of the writing assignment. They also learn how to use new grammatical structures in a meaningful context. Finally, they focus on editing and proofreading their writing for grammatical and mechanical correctness.

DESIGN OF THE UNITS

The units are closely linked to the content of *NorthStar: Focus on Reading and Writing*. Therefore, it is essential that the books be used together. Each *Writing Activity Book* unit contains four sections that follow the writing process: Prewriting, Organizing, Revising, and Editing. The assignments are drawn from topics discussed in the Student Book readings and subsequent exercises. Teachers can choose to complete an entire unit in the Student Book before starting the writing unit. Alternatively, they can begin the Prewriting activities after completing the indicated sections in the Student Book and finish both units together. Checklists for the first, second, and final drafts remind students of which points to focus on in each draft.

1. Prewriting

Students complete Sections 1–4 in the Student Book before they begin this section. The activities in this section help students generate ideas and narrow a topic. They learn how to use a variety of prewriting techniques, such as interviewing, listing, and making charts. Typically, students work together to analyze and manipulate a model prewriting exercise. Then they try using the prewriting technique on their own.

2. Organizing

In this section, students focus on organizing and developing their ideas. They learn about a structural or rhetorical feature of writing, such as writing topic and supporting sentences or organizing around a rhetorical feature. They may analyze a model paragraph or organize ideas from the readings. Then they apply the ideas to their own writing. At the end of this section, students complete the first draft of the assignment and do a peer review exercise.

3. Revising

The activities in this section are designed to help students expand and polish their writing. The section has two parts. Part A, which is often drawn from Section 6B: Style in the Student Book, focuses on developing the content of students' writing. The activities help students achieve coherence and unity in their writing and clarify and improve the support for their ideas. Part B, which is often drawn from Section 6A: Grammar in the Student Book, helps students use the grammar point in a meaningful way in their writing. Students do exercises that use the grammar point in context. Then they look for places to apply the grammar in their writing. Although attention is given to grammatical correctness, meaningful usage is the focus. At the end of this section, students write the second draft of the assignment.

4. Editing

In this section, students focus on editing their writing for grammar, form, and mechanics. They focus on editing one feature, often drawn from Section 6B: Style in the Student Book. They identify and practice editing the feature in controlled exercises and then look for errors in their own writing. At the end of this section, students finish the final draft of the assignment.

THE FRIENDSHIP PAGE

OVERVIEW

Theme:	**Friendship**
Prewriting:	**Interviewing**
Organizing:	**Ordering your ideas**
Revising:	**Using adjectives** **Using the simple present of *be***
Editing:	**Writing a sentence**

Assignment

◆ **Interview a classmate.**

◆ **Write sentences about your classmate and your classmate's friend.**

---

1 PREWRITING

INTERVIEWING

 First, complete Unit 1, Sections 1–4 and 6A, in the Student Book. Then, begin this section.

Interviewing is one way to learn about another person. In an interview, you ask a person questions. You can use the information from the interview when you write.

❶ *Write questions to ask your classmate. Use the verb* be. *The first one is done for you.*

1. What/your name   **What is your name?** _____

2. Where/you from _____

3. How old/you _____

4. What/your job _____

5. What/your hobbies or interests _____

6. Who/your best friend _____

7. Where/he (or she) from _____

8. How old/he (or she) _____

9. What/his (or her) job _____

10. What/his (or her) hobbies or interests _____

2 *Interview a classmate. Ask the questions from Exercise 1. Write the answers on a separate piece of paper. Write complete sentences.*

ORGANIZING

ORDERING YOUR IDEAS

When you write, you can order your ideas in different ways. The descriptions below are both correct, but the ideas are in a different order.

1 *Read Description 1. It gives sentences about Fernando and then sentences about his friend, Ricardo.*

Description 1

My classmate's name is Fernando. He is from Spain. He is 21 years old. He is a student in Chicago. Fernando is friendly. He likes going to parties. Fernando's best friend is Ricardo. He is from Spain. He is 20 years old. He is a student in Madrid. Ricardo is friendly and athletic. He likes going to parties and playing sports.

2 *Read Description 2. It gives one sentence about Fernando, then one sentence about Ricardo, two sentences about Fernando, then two sentences about Ricardo.*

Description 2

> My classmate's name is Fernando. His best friend is Ricardo. Fernando is from Spain. He is 21 years old. Ricardo is also from Spain. He is 20 years old. Fernando is a student in Chicago. Ricardo is a student in Madrid. Fernando and Ricardo are both friendly. They like going to parties. Ricardo also likes playing sports.

3 *Read Description 1 and Description 2 again. For both descriptions:*

- *underline the sentences about Fernando.*
- *circle the sentences about Ricardo.*
- *underline and circle the sentences about both Fernando and Ricardo.*

4 *Look at your sentences from Prewriting, Exercise 2, on page 2. Order your ideas. Number the sentences. You can organize your sentences like Description 1 or Description 2.*

Writing the First Draft

Your first draft is the first time you write your ideas. Your first draft will be different from your final draft. You will make some changes. Now you are ready to write your first draft.

Begin like this: "My classmate's name is. . . . He is. . . ."

OR like this: "My classmate's name is. . . . His best friend is. . . ."

Don't worry about grammar. Just try to make your ideas clear.

PEER REVIEW

Work with a partner (not the classmate you interviewed). Read your partner's first draft. Answer the question below. Then discuss your answers with your partner.

What does the writer include? Check (✓) the information.

	Classmate	Classmate's friend
Age	_____	_____
Job	_____	_____
Hobbies	_____	_____
Other	_____	_____

REVISING

A. USING ADJECTIVES

 First, complete Unit 1, Section 5A, in the Student Book. Then, begin this section.

Adjectives can describe a person.

Fernando is **friendly**. He likes to meet new people.

1 *Look back at the description in Organizing, Exercise 1, on page 2. What sentences have adjectives? Put a star (✱) next to the sentences that use adjectives.*

2 *Match each adjective with its meaning. The first one is done for you.*

Adjectives to describe people

_**b**_ 1. athletic	**a.**	likes to meet new people
_____ 2. talkative	**b.**	able to play a sport very well
_____ 3. helpful	**c.**	makes people laugh
_____ 4. shy	**d.**	is nervous around new people
_____ 5. popular	**e.**	able to wait for something without getting upset
_____ 6. friendly	**f.**	helps other people
_____ 7. patient	**g.**	someone many people like
_____ 8. funny	**h.**	can learn and understand things quickly
_____ 9. intelligent	**i.**	likes to talk a lot
_____10. honest	**j.**	does not lie

3 *Work with the class. What other adjectives describe people? Write them down on a separate piece of paper.*

Do the adjectives have positive (good) or negative (bad) meanings? Write (+) next to those that are positive and (−) next to those that are negative.

Example

   unfriendly (−)   nice (+)

4 *Work with the classmate you interviewed in Prewriting, Exercise 2, on page 2. Is there anything else you want to know about your classmate or your classmate's friend? Ask your classmate one or two more questions. What adjectives can you use to describe your classmate and your classmate's friend? Write one sentence about each person. Add it to your description.*

B. USING THE SIMPLE PRESENT OF *Be*

 First, complete Unit 1, Section 6A, in the Student Book. Then, begin this section.

Use the verb *be* to describe people.

I **am** talkative.

He/She **is** helpful.

You/We/They **are** intelligent.

❶ *Complete the sentences. Use the verb* be. *The first one is done for you.*

1. My classmate's name _____**is**_____ Alice.

2. Alice _____ from Taiwan.

3. She _____ funny and intelligent.

4. Her friend's name _____ Irani.

5. Irani _____ from Brazil.

6. Irani _____ a friendly person.

7. Alice and Irani _____ students.

8. They _____ both interested in music.

❷ *Look at the sentences in Exercise 1 again. Check (✓) the sentences with adjectives.*

❸ *Look at the sentences in your first draft. Do you use the verb* be *to describe your classmate and his or her friend? Underline the verb* be. *Make sure you use the correct form.*

Writing the Second Draft

Now you are ready to write your second draft. Look at your first draft. Be sure you:

◆ describe your classmate and his or her friend.

◆ add adjectives if necessary.

◆ use the simple present of *be* correctly.

Now, rewrite your first draft.

EDITING

WRITING A SENTENCE

 First, complete Unit 1, Section 6B, in the Student Book. Then, begin this section.

Read the rules for writing a sentence.

◆ A sentence is a group of words that expresses a complete idea.

◆ A sentence must have a subject and a verb.

◆ The first word in a sentence must begin with a capital letter.

◆ Use a period (.), exclamation point (!), or question mark (?) at the end of a sentence.

1 *Read the sentences. Six sentences have errors. Correct the errors. The first one is done for you.*

> **M**
> (1) ~~my~~ classmate's name is Bernard. (2) He is 24 years old. (3) He is from Senegal (4) Likes playing soccer and going out dancing. (5) Bernard's friend Alexandre. (6) He is from France. (7) He intelligent and shy. (8) he likes going to the beach and reading.

2 *Look at your second draft. Are the sentences correct? Correct any errors in the sentences.*

Preparing the Final Draft

Carefully edit your second draft. Use the checklist below. Then neatly write or type your sentences with the corrections.

FINAL DRAFT CHECKLIST

❑ Do you describe a classmate and his or her best friend?

❑ Do you order your ideas clearly?

❑ Do you use adjectives to describe people?

❑ Do you use the verb *be* correctly?

❑ Are the sentences correct?

ART FOR EVERYONE

OVERVIEW

Theme:	**The arts**
Prewriting:	**Finding information in a reading**
Organizing:	**Writing a biography**
Revising:	**Using dates** **Using the simple past of** *be*
Editing:	**Using commas**

Assignment

◆ **Write a biography of Keith Haring.**

---

1 PREWRITING

FINDING INFORMATION IN A READING

 First, complete Unit 2, Sections 1–4, in the Student Book. Then, begin this section.

A biography is the story of a person's life. For this assignment, you will use the information in *Reading One: Art for Everyone* to write a biography of Keith Haring.

❶ *Look at the timeline in Section 3A in the Student Book. Then answer the questions on page 8 about Keith Haring. The first one is done for you. The second one is started for you.*

1. Where and when was Keith Haring born?

   <u>Keith Haring was born in Kutztown, Pennsylvania, in 1958.</u>

2. When did Haring die?

   <u>He died</u>

3. When was Haring arrested by police? Why was he arrested?

   _____

4. When was Haring an art student? Where?

   _____

5. What were Haring's first drawings? Where were they?

   _____

6. When and where was Haring's first important art show?

   _____

2 *Find one more thing about Haring in Reading One that you think is interesting. Write it below. Include this in your biography of Keith Haring.*

_____

ORGANIZING

WRITING A BIOGRAPHY

A biography describes a person. It also tells when important events happened in the person's life. A biography usually gives events in time order (the order they happened). The writer begins with the earliest event and ends with the last event.

1 *Read the sentences about Andy Warhol. Number the sentences in time order from 1 to 7. The first one is done for you.*

_____ **a.** Warhol was a student at Carnegie Institute of Technology from 1945 to 1949.

_____ **b.** Andy Warhol and Keith Haring were good friends in the 1980s.

_____ **c.** Andy Warhol died in 1987.

_____ **d.** By the early 1960s, Andy Warhol was a famous Pop artist.

__1__ **e.** Andy Warhol was born in Pennsylvania in 1912.

_____ **f.** In the 1950s, Warhol was a commercial artist on Madison Ave. in New York.

_____ **g.** Warhol had his first art show in 1952.

2 *Work with a partner. Compare your answers for Exercise 1. Were your answers the same as your partner's? Talk about any differences.*

3 *Look at your answers to the questions about Keith Haring in Prewriting, Exercise 1, on page 8. Put them in time order.*

Writing the First Draft

Use the information from Prewriting, Exercise 1, on page 8 to write your first draft.

* Write complete sentences about Keith Haring.

* Begin your first sentence "Keith Haring was born . . . "

* Begin your last sentence "Keith Haring died . . . "

* Put your sentences in time order.

Don't worry about grammar. Just try to make your ideas clear.

PEER REVIEW

Work with a partner. Read your partner's first draft. Answer the questions below. Then discuss your answers with your partner.

* Did the writer use information from the reading in the biography?

* Are the ideas in time order? Circle any sentences you think should be moved to another place.

REVISING

A. USING DATES

Using dates helps put your ideas in time order. Dates tell when something happened.

For example:

in **1963**

from **1963** to **1965**

Dates can come at the beginning or end of a sentence. At the beginning of a sentence, dates are followed by a comma. At the end of a sentence, you don't need a comma.

For example:

In 1952, he had his first art show in New York.

He had his first art show in New York **in 1952.**

1 *Read the timeline about Robert Rauschenberg, another American Pop artist. Then read the beginning of his biography. Complete the biography with the correct dates from the box. The first one is done for you.*

Timeline of Robert Rauschenberg's Life

Year	Event
1925	Rauschenberg is born in Port Arthur, Texas.
1942	He studies at the University of Texas.
1947–1948	He studies music, sculpture, and art at the Kansas City Art Institute.
1949	He moves to New York City.
1951	Rauschenberg has his first art show.
1953	He makes art for a dance company. He uses light and sound in his art.
1998	The Guggenheim Museum shows Rauschenberg's art.
Today	Rauschenberg's art is in public collections around the world. People call him the "Father of Pop Art."

1948	1951	1942	1947	~~1925~~

Biography of Robert Rauschenberg

Rauschenberg was born in Port Arthur, Texas, in _____1925_____. In _____,
                                                        1.   2.
he was a student at the University of Texas. He was a student and studied art at

the Kansas City Art Institute from _____ to _____. His first
                                              3.   4.
important show was in New York City in _____. Today, people call him
                                                  5.
the "Father of Pop Art."

2 *Look again at the biography of Robert Rauschenberg. Find examples of:*

1. a date at the beginning of a sentence. Circle it.

2. a date at the end of a sentence. Underline it.

3 *Look at the first draft of your biography. Do you use dates at the beginning and end of sentences? Rewrite some sentences. Include dates at the beginning of some sentences and at the end of other sentences.*

B. USING THE SIMPLE PAST OF *Be*

First, complete Unit 2, Section 6A, in the Student Book. Then, begin this section.

1 *Complete the sentences with the simple past of* be. *Use the negative form in the last sentence. The first one is done for you.*

1. Keith Haring and Andy Warhol _____**were**_____ Pop artists.

2. Their drawings _____ controversial.

3. Warhol _____ an art student from 1945 to 1949.

4. Robert Rauschenberg's first art show _____ in New York.

5. Some of his art _____ about city life.

6. Some of Warhol's art _____ of famous people.

7. Warhol _____ also a filmmaker and writer.

8. Keith Haring _____ a filmmaker or a writer.

2 *Look at the first draft of your biography. Make sure you use the simple past of* be *correctly.*

Writing the Second Draft

Now you are ready to write your second draft. Look at your first draft. Be sure you:

♦ use dates at the beginning of some sentences and at the end of other sentences.

♦ use the simple past of *be* correctly.

Now, rewrite your first draft.

4 EDITING
USING COMMAS

First, complete Unit 2, Section 6B, in the Student Book. Then, begin this section.

Read the rules for using commas:

1. Use a comma after words like *For example* and *Finally.*
2. Use a comma after a date at the beginning of a sentence.
3. Use a comma to join two small sentences with *and, but,* and *or.*
4. Use a comma to separate the names of cities from the names of states or countries.
5. Use a comma to separate things in a list.

1 *Read the biography of another American Pop artist, Roy Lichtenstein. Six commas are missing from the paragraph. Add the commas.*

> Roy Lichtenstein was born in New York in 1923. From 1946 to 1949 he was an art student at Ohio State University in Columbus Ohio. His first art show was in 1951. He made paintings drawings and sculptures. Some of his paintings were very popular. For example his most popular paintings were cartoons. His art is in museums all over the world and he is still very famous. Lichtenstein died in 1997.

2 *Look at your second draft. Make sure you use commas correctly.*

Preparing the Final Draft

Carefully edit your second draft. Use the checklist below. Then neatly write or type your biography with the corrections.

FINAL DRAFT CHECKLIST

❑ Do you use information from the reading to write a biography of Keith Haring?

❑ Is the information organized in time order?

❑ Do you use dates at the beginning of some sentences, and at the end of other sentences?

❑ Do you use the past tense of *be* correctly?

❑ Are the sentences correct?

❑ Do you use commas correctly?

WHAT'S IT WORTH TO YOU?

OVERVIEW

Theme: **Special possessions**

Prewriting: **Questioning yourself**

Organizing: **Writing topic sentences**

Revising: **Staying on the topic**
                  Using the simple present

Editing: **Formatting a paragraph**

Assignment

◆ **Write a paragraph.**

◆ **Describe a special possession.**

◆ **Explain why it is important to you.**

1   PREWRITING

QUESTIONING YOURSELF

First, complete Unit 3, Sections 1–4, in the Student Book. Then, begin this section.

You can get ideas for your writing by asking yourself questions about the topic.

1 *Think of some special possessions or collections that you have. Make a list of four or five items. A special possession can be something that:*

- *you collect.*
- *you received as a gift.*
- *helps you remember a special person, event, or time in your life.*

See the example on page 14.

13

Example

My Special Possessions
○ my high school soccer shirt
family photographs
grandfather's painting
○ Beatles collection

2 *Choose two special possessions from the list you made. Complete the chart.*

	Possession 1	**Possession 2**
1. What is your special possession?		
2. Where did you get it?		
3. How much is it worth?		
4. Why do you keep it?		

3 *Choose one possession to write about.*

ORGANIZING

WRITING TOPIC SENTENCES

A paragraph is a group of sentences about one main idea. The first sentence usually gives the main idea of the paragraph. It is called a topic sentence. The other sentences explain or support the topic sentence.

1 *Read the paragraph. Underline the topic sentence.*

One of my special possessions is my collection of family photographs. I have hundreds of photos. I have very old photos of my great-grandparents. I also have wedding photos of my grandparents. I especially love the photos of my parents when they were children. Sometimes I spend hours looking at the pictures. I like the photos because my family is very important to me.

2 *Read the paragraph. It is missing the topic sentence. Read the topic sentences below the paragraph. Choose the best topic sentence and write it on the line.*

_____. It is yellow and black and has the number "11." It also has my name on the back. I got it in high school when I played on the school team. Our team won every game. The shirt has a lot of sentimental value. I keep it because I like to remember my teammates. We were good friends. We had a lot of fun.

Topic Sentences

    a. My team won the soccer championship in high school.

    b. My high school soccer shirt is very special to me.

    c. Soccer is my favorite sport.

3 *Look back at Prewriting, Exercise 3, on page 14. What special possession are you going to write about? Write a topic sentence for your paragraph.*

Writing the First Draft

Now you are ready to write your first draft.

* Include a topic sentence that gives the main idea of your paragraph.

* Write sentences to explain or support the main idea.

Don't worry about grammar. Just try to make your ideas clear.

PEER REVIEW

Work with a partner. Read your partner's first draft. Answer the questions below. Then discuss your answers with your partner.

* Does the paragraph have a topic sentence? Underline it.

* Put a check (✓) next to the questions that are answered in the paragraph:

    ❑ What is the writer's special possession?

    ❑ What does it look like?

    ❑ Where did the writer get it?

    ❑ How much is it worth?

    ❑ Why does the writer keep it?

REVISING

A. STAYING ON THE TOPIC

All the sentences in a paragraph explain and support the main idea. Sentences about other topics do not belong.

❶ *Read the paragraph. The topic sentence is underlined. One sentence is not about the main idea. It is crossed out.*

> <u>One of my special possessions is a painting by my grandfather.</u> He was not a professional painter, but he painted as a hobby. ~~My sister also paints~~. My favorite painting is a picture of the house where my grandfather grew up. The house is yellow and there are trees around it. My grandfather gave me the picture before he died. I think of him every time I look at the picture.

❷ *Read the paragraph. Underline the topic sentence. Cross out one sentence that is not about the main idea. Work with a partner. Explain why you chose that sentence to cross out.*

> My bicycle is a very special possession. My bike is not worth a lot of money. It is old, but it is in good condition. I ride my bike every day. I ride it to school, to the store, and to visit my friends. I also know how to drive a car. I can go wherever I want because I have a bike.

❸ *Look at the first draft of your paragraph. Do all the sentences explain and support the topic sentence? Cross out sentences that are not about the main idea. If necessary, write new sentences.*

B. USING THE SIMPLE PRESENT

 First, complete Unit 3, Section 6A, in the Student Book. Then, begin this section.

The simple present tense describes facts and things that are always true. You can use the simple present tense to describe your special possession and why it is important to you.

1 *Complete the paragraph. Write the simple present tense of each verb on the line. The first one is done for you.*

My most important possession _____is_____ my collection of Beatles music.
                                                 1. be

I _____ almost one hundred Beatles CDs. My collection also
   2. own

_____ Beatles books and posters. I _____ how much my
   3. include   4. not know

collection is worth. However, I do not want to sell it. I _____ listening to
                                                       5. enjoy

the Beatles. I _____ to own every recording they made.
        6. want

2 *Read the paragraph. The six <u>underlined</u> verbs are incorrect. Correct the verbs. The first one is done for you.*

                                is
My most special possession ~~are~~ my favorite cookbook. My favorite cookbook <u>are</u> from my grandmother. It <u>have</u> recipes that she made for me when I was a child. I also <u>having</u> cookbooks from all over the world. I <u>likes</u> to taste new kinds of food. My cookbook collection <u>give</u> me a lot of ideas for new recipes.

3 *Look at the first draft of your paragraph. Underline all the simple present tense verbs. Make sure you use the correct form of each simple present tense verb.*

Writing the Second Draft

Now you are ready to write your second draft. Look at your first draft. Be sure you:

◆ begin with a good topic sentence.

◆ use sentences to explain or support the topic sentence.

◆ use the correct form of simple present tense verbs.

Now, rewrite your first draft.

EDITING
FORMATTING A PARAGRAPH

 First, complete Unit 3, Section 6B, in the Student Book. Then, begin this exercise.

1 *Look at the two paragraphs below. Did the writer follow the rules for formatting each paragraph correctly? Circle* Yes *or* No. *The first one is done for you.*

Did the writer . . .	Paragraph 1		Paragraph 2	
◆ indent the first line of the paragraph?	Yes	(No)	Yes	No
◆ write between the left and right margins?	Yes	No	Yes	No
◆ begin new sentences on the same line?	Yes	No	Yes	No

Paragraph 1

> My Special Possession
>
> The shirt from my soccer team is very special to me.
>
> It is yellow and black and has the number "11." It also has my name on the back.
>
> I got it in high school when I played on the school team. Our team won every game.
>
> The shirt has a lot of sentimental value.
>
> I keep it because I like to remember the team. We were good friends and had a lot of fun.

Paragraph 2

> My Special Possession
>
> The shirt from my soccer team is very special to me. It is yellow and black and has the number "11." It also has my name on the back. I got it in high school when I played on the school team. Our team won every game. The shirt has a lot of sentimental value. I keep it because I like to remember the team. We were good friends and had a lot of fun.

2 *Look at your second draft. Does it have the correct format? Put a check (✓) next to each rule you followed.*

❑ Indent the first line of the paragraph.

❑ Write between the left and right margins on your paper.

❑ Do not start each sentence on a new line.

Preparing the Final Draft

Carefully edit your second draft. Use the checklist below. Then neatly write or type your paragraph with the corrections.

FINAL DRAFT CHECKLIST

❑ Is the paragraph about a special possession?

❑ Do you include a topic sentence that gives the main idea?

❑ Do all the other sentences explain and support your main idea?

❑ Do you use the simple present tense correctly?

❑ Do you format the paragraph correctly?

STRENGTH IN NUMBERS

OVERVIEW

Theme: Strength in numbers

Prewriting: Listing

Organizing: Writing a letter to the editor

Revising: Introducing examples
              Using pronouns and possessive adjectives

Editing: Formatting a letter

Assignment

♦ Write a letter to the editor of a local newspaper.

♦ Explain who you are and why you support a group that helps
  your community.

1 PREWRITING

LISTING

*First, complete Unit 4, Sections 1–4, in the Student Book.
Then, begin this section.*

Sometimes it helps to make a list before you start writing. When
you make a list, you do not have to write complete sentences.

❶ *Work with the class. Make a list of organizations that help your
community. Think of organizations that help children or
teenagers, like the Urban Angels or DAREArts. Think of other
organizations that support or teach about art, music, drama,
science, sports, or a hobby. Think of organizations that support
animals, health, social issues, or religion. Write them on the list.*

Community Organizations	Who or What They Help
Urban Angels, DAREarts	children or teenagers
	art, music, or drama
	science
	sports
	hobby
	animals
	health
	social issues
	religion
	other

2 *Choose one organization to write about on a separate piece of paper. Make a list of all the ways the organization helps your community.*

Example

Urban Angels
• help teens stay in school
• help teens avoid drugs, gangs, guns, crime
• go to museums
• visit businesses
• have afterschool and weekend activities
• take classes and learn about social issues
• learn to be role models

ORGANIZING

WRITING A LETTER TO THE EDITOR

People write letters to the editor because they want to share their opinions with the community. Letters to the editor are in the newspaper for everyone to read.

Letters to the editor should explain:

◆ who you are (Are you a student? A teacher? A police officer?)

◆ which community organization you are writing about.

◆ why you support the organization.

❶ *Read the letter to the editor. Then, read the questions and the answers below.*

Letter to the Editor

March 18, 2003

Dear Editor,

    I am a student in New York City. I am writing about an organization called the Urban Angels. The Urban Angels help teenagers avoid problems such as drugs, crime, and gangs. They want teenagers to stay in school. The Urban Angels have activities after school and on weekends. In addition, the Urban Angels help the community. Teenagers can take classes about social issues. They learn how to take care of themselves and stop problems in the community. Finally, the Urban Angels help their city. For example, they paint over graffiti at neighborhood "paint-outs." At park cleanups, they go to city parks and make them beautiful again. For all these reasons, I think people should support the Urban Angels.

                           Sincerely,

                           Maurice Roberts

1. Who is writing the letter? (Who is Maurice Roberts?)

   A student from New York City

2. Which community group is he writing about?

   He's writing about the Urban Angels.

3. Why does he support the group?

   He supports the Urban Angels because they help teenagers avoid problems

   and stay in school. They also help their community and their city.

2 *Read the letter to the editor. Then, answer the questions.*

Letter to the Editor

September 10, 2004

Dear Editor,

I am a high school art teacher. I am writing about the Neighborhood Art Center. The Neighborhood Art Center has art classes for children and adults. Children can take art classes after school. There are classes for adults in the evenings and on weekends. In addition, the Art Center supports local artists. Local artists teach the classes at the Art Center. The Art Center gift shop sells paintings and other art by local artists. For all these reasons, I think people should support the Art Center.

Sincerely,

Maude Moran

1. Who is Maude Moran?

   _____

2. Which community organization is she writing about?

   _____

3. Why does she support the organization?

   _____

3 *Think about the organization you chose in Prewriting, Exercise 2, on page 21. Read your list of ways the organization helps your community. Choose two or three ways to include in your letter.*

Writing the First Draft

Now you are ready to write your first draft.

* Say who you are (a student, a teacher, a police officer).
* Say what community organization you are writing about.
* Explain why you support the organization.

Don't worry about grammar. Just try to make your ideas clear.

PEER REVIEW

Work with a partner. Read your partner's first draft. Answer the questions below. Then discuss your answers with your partner.

◆ Who is the writer?

◆ Which community organization does the writer support?

◆ Why does the writer support the organization?

◆ Ask your partner one question about the organization.

---

3 REVISING

A. INTRODUCING EXAMPLES

Giving examples is a good way to support an opinion. There are several ways to introduce examples.

Use *such as* to introduce examples in a sentence. A list of things often follows *such as*.

The Urban Angels help teenagers avoid problems **such as** drugs, crimes, and gangs.

Use *for example* to introduce an example in a new sentence. A comma and a complete sentence follow *for example*.

The Urban Angels help the city. **For example,** they paint over graffiti at neighborhood "paint-outs."

1 *Look back at the letter in Organizing, Exercise 1, on page 22. Underline the sentences with* such as *and* for example.

2 *Read the statements and examples about the Neighborhood Art Center. Rewrite each statement and example in one or two complete sentences. Introduce each example with* such as *or* for example. *The first two are done for you.*

1. *Statement:*   The Neighborhood Art Center helps children.

   Example: Children can learn about art.

   Complete sentence(s): <u>The Neighborhood Art Center helps children. For</u>
   <u>example, children can learn about art.</u>

2. *Statement:*   The Neighborhood Art Center has many art classes.

Example: painting, drawing, and sculpture

Complete sentence(s): <u>The Neighborhood Art Center has many art classes</u>
<u>such as painting, drawing, and sculpture.</u>

3. *Statement:*   The Neighborhood Art Center has classes for all ages.

Example: children, college students, adults, and senior citizens

Complete sentence(s): _____

_____

4. *Statement:*   The art classes are not expensive.

Example: A drawing class costs only $15 per semester.

Complete sentence(s): _____

_____

5. *Statement:*   The Neighborhood Art Center supports local artists.

Example: Local artists teach classes at the Art Center.

Complete sentence(s): _____

_____

6. *Statement:*   The gift shop sells art by local artists.

Example: jewelry, paintings, and pottery

Complete sentence(s): _____

_____

B. USING PRONOUNS AND POSSESSIVE ADJECTIVES

 First, complete Unit 4, Section 6A, in the Student Book. Then, begin this section.

♦ A pronoun *(he, she, it, they)* takes the place of a noun. When you do not want to repeat a noun in a sentence, use a pronoun.

♦ A possessive adjective *(his, her, its, their)* shows ownership. Possessive adjectives always come before a noun.

❶ *Look at the sentences on page 26. Draw an arrow from each underlined pronoun or possessive adjective to the noun it refers to.*

1. The Urban Angels help teenagers avoid problems. <u>They</u> want teenagers to stay in school.

2. Teenagers can take classes about social issues. <u>They</u> learn how to take care of themselves.

3. The Urban Angels help their city. <u>They</u> paint over graffiti at neighborhood "paint-outs." At park cleanups, <u>they</u> go to city parks and make <u>them</u> beautiful again.

❷ *Read the letter. Complete each sentence with* it, they, them, *or* their.

Letter to the Editor

July 31, 2003

Dear Editor,

I am a student at the local community college. I am writing about the Senior

Center. _____It_____ helps many older people in our community. The Senior Center
　　　　　　1.

helps elderly people stay healthy. _____ can take exercises classes such as
　　　　　　　　　　　　　　　　　　　　　2.

swimming, walking, and aerobics. Doctors come to the center weekly to check

_____ health. In addition, the Senior Center bus helps older people get
　　　3.

around town. For example, _____ takes _____ to the shopping
　　　　　　　　　　　　　　　　4.　　　　　　　　　　5.

center. _____ also goes to places such as museums and movie theaters.
　　　　　6.

Finally, the Senior Center helps seniors stay involved in the community. For example,

_____ can volunteer at a local school. _____ read to the children
　　　7.　　　　　　　　　　　　　　　　　　　　　　8.

and help _____ with homework. For all these reasons, I think the Senior
　　　　　　9.

Center is important for our community.

Sincerely,

Ji-Lan Li

---

❸ *Look at the first draft of your letter. Underline all the pronouns and possessive adjectives. Make sure you use them correctly.*

Writing the Second Draft

Now you are ready to write your second draft. Look at your first draft. Be sure you:

◆　use *for example* and *such as* to introduce examples.

◆　use pronouns and possessive adjectives correctly.

Now, rewrite your first draft.

EDITING
FORMATTING A LETTER

1 *Look at the letter to the editor. Circle and label the five parts of the letter:* date, greeting, message, closing, and signature. *The first one is done for you.*

Letter to the Editor

<u>March 18, 2003</u> **date**

Dear Editor,

   I am a student in New York City. I am writing about an organization called the Urban Angels. The Urban Angels help teenagers avoid problems such as drugs, crime, and gangs. They want teenagers to stay in school. The Urban Angels have activities after school and on weekends. In addition, the Urban Angels help the community. Teenagers can take classes about social issues. They learn how to take care of themselves and stop problems in the community. Finally, the Urban Angels help their city. For example, they paint over graffiti at neighborhood "paint-outs." At park cleanups, they go to city parks and make them beautiful again. For all these reasons, I think people should support the Urban Angels.

   Sincerely,

   Maurice Roberts

---

2 *Look at your second draft. Does it include the five parts of a letter? Add any missing parts.*

Preparing the Final Draft

Carefully edit your second draft. Use the checklist below. Then neatly write or type your letter with the corrections.

FINAL DRAFT CHECKLIST

❑ Is your letter about an organization that helps your community?

❑ Do you say who you are?

❑ Do you include examples to support your opinion?

❑ Do you use *such as* and *for example* to introduce your examples?

❑ Do you use pronouns and possessive adjectives correctly?

❑ Do you format the letter correctly?

GOING OUT OF BUSINESS

OVERVIEW

Theme:	Business
Prewriting:	Drawing a picture
Organizing:	Describing a place
Revising:	Using spatial descriptions Using *There is/ There are*
Editing:	Correcting subject-verb agreement

Assignment

◆ Write a paragraph.

◆ Describe a store or restaurant.

1 PREWRITING

DRAWING A PICTURE

 First, complete Unit 5, Sections 1–4, in the Student Book. Then, begin this section.

Drawing a picture helps you remember what a place looks like. It can also help you organize your ideas.

1 *Work with a partner. Talk about the stores and restaurants you like. Here are some places. Write one example of each place. The first one is done for you.*

Places	Examples
Restaurant	<u>The Big Salad</u>
Department store	
Video store	
Clothing store	
Grocery (food) store	
Bookstore	
Other	

2 *Work with a partner. Look at the picture of The Big Salad. Answer the questions.*

1. What kind of place is The Big Salad?

   _____

2. Where is it? What is nearby?

   _____

3 *Look at your list from Exercise 1 at the top of this page. Choose one place to write about. Draw a map of the store or restaurant on a separate piece of paper. Draw the things inside and the area around it.*

4 *Work with a partner. Look at your partner's map and ask your partner the questions. Then, your partner will ask you the questions about your map.*

1. What place is the writer describing?

2. Where is it? What is nearby?

3. What does it sell?

4. What is the atmosphere (the feeling inside the place) like?

5. Why do you like it?

ORGANIZING
DESCRIBING A PLACE

When you describe a place, you can use words that describe how things look, feel, smell, taste, or sound.

1 *Read the paragraph. Work with a partner. Answer the questions.*

> I like The Big Salad. The Big Salad is on Main Street. It is next to the post office and across from the department store. When you walk in the door, you smell fresh bread. There is a large salad bar. There are also tasty soups, such as chicken noodle, clam chowder, and onion. I also like the atmosphere. There are big windows in the front. It is very bright and cheerful. The Big Salad is a great place to eat.

1. What place is the writer describing?

2. Where is it? What is nearby?

3. What does it sell?

4. What is the atmosphere like?

5. Why does the writer like it?

2 *Read the paragraph again. Make a list of the descriptive words. The list is started for you.*

   fresh   _____   _____   _____

   large   _____   _____

3 *Complete the paragraph with the descriptive words below. The first one is done for you.*

big	~~interesting~~	near my house
comfortable	next to the window	friendly

The Night Owl Bookshop is a great place to buy books. It is open late at night. It

has a lot of ____interesting____ books. For example, it has a _____
                        1.   2.

selection of comic books. I also like the atmosphere in the Night Owl. There are a

lot of _____ chairs. My favorite chair is _____. The
                 3.   4.

employees are very _____. They always say hello. I'm glad that The
                             5.

Night Owl Bookshop is _____.
                                  6.

Writing the First Draft

Now you are ready to write your first draft.

◆   Write a paragraph describing a store or restaurant you like.

◆   Write a topic sentence. Be sure it gives the name of the store or restaurant and tells
     why you like it.

◆   Use descriptive words.

Don't worry about grammar. Just try to make your ideas clear.

PEER REVIEW

Work with a partner. Read your partner's first draft. Answer the questions below.
Then discuss your answers with your partner.

◆ What place is the writer describing?

◆ Why does the writer like it?

◆ Ask your partner one question about the store or restaurant.

REVISING

A. USING SPATIAL DESCRIPTIONS

 First, complete Unit 5, Section 6B, in the Student Book. Then, begin this section.

You can use spatial descriptions to explain where things are. Use prepositions such as *between, next to, on,* and *across from.*

① *Look back at the map in Prewriting, Exercise 2, on page 29. Complete the sentences. Circle the correct preposition. The first one is done for you.*

1. The Big Salad is *(at /(on)* Main Street.

2. The Big Salad is *(across from / next to)* the bank.

3. It is *(between / around the corner from)* the post office and the bank.

4. The front door of The Big Salad is *(behind / around the corner from)* the post office.

5. The Big Salad is *(behind / across from)* the department store.

6. There are tables *(between / in front of)* the big windows.

7. The salad bar is *(around the corner from / to the right of)* the cashier.

8. The cashier is *(on / in front of)* the front door.

② *Look at the first draft of your paragraph. Do you use spatial descriptions to describe location? If not, add one or two spatial descriptions to your paragraph. Describe the location of the store or restaurant and what it looks like inside.*

B. USING *There is / There are*

 First, complete Unit 5, Section 6A, in the Student Book. Then, begin this section.

Use *there is* or *there are* to describe a place in the present tense.

① *Look back at the paragraph about The Big Salad restaurant in Organizing, Exercise 1, on page 30. Underline the sentences with* there is *or* there are.

2 *Complete the sentences with* there is *or* there are. *Underline the noun in each sentence. Then put a check (✓) in the column under singular count noun, plural count noun, or non-count noun. The first one is done for you.*

		Singular count noun	Plural count noun	Non-count noun
1. __There are__	two <u>cafés</u> nearby.	❑	☑	❑
2. _____	soft music playing.	❑	❑	❑
3. _____	delicious ice cream.	❑	❑	❑
4. _____	some tables outside.	❑	❑	❑
5. _____	a salad bar.	❑	❑	❑
6. _____	a comfortable chair.	❑	❑	❑

3 *Look at the first draft of your paragraph. Do you use* there is *or* there are *to describe the place? If not, add one or two sentences with* there is *or* there are.

Writing the Second Draft

Now you are ready to write your second draft. Look at your first draft. Be sure you:

- Use spatial descriptions. Describe the location of the store or restaurant. Use prepositions of location correctly.

- Use *there is* or *there are.*

Now, rewrite your first draft.

EDITING

CORRECTING SUBJECT-VERB AGREEMENT

A verb must agree with its subject. It must agree in person and number.

Example

S V
My sister likes to shop.

S V
They are very friendly.

1 *Read the paragraph. Circle the correct verb forms. The first one is done for you.*

I _____*go*_____ shopping at the farmer's market every week. I
    1. go / goes

_____ shopping there. The food _____ very fresh.
2. like / likes   3. is / are

There are about ten farm stands in the market. Near the entrance, there are

several vegetable stands. They _____ many different kinds of
                       4. sell / sells

vegetables. There is also a fruit stand. It _____ fresh fruit from
                       5. sell / sells

local farms. The fruit _____ very good. The prices
               6. is / are

_____ very low. I buy all my fruit and vegetables from the
7. is / are

farmer's market.

2 *Look at your second draft. Underline the verbs. Make sure the verbs agree with their subjects.*

Preparing the Final Draft

Carefully edit your second draft. Use the checklist below. Then neatly write or type your paragraph with the corrections.

FINAL DRAFT CHECKLIST

❏ Do you describe a store or restaurant?

❏ Do you include a topic sentence?

❏ Do you describe how things look, feel, taste, smell, and sound?

❏ Do you use prepositions to describe where things are?

❏ Do you use *there is* or *there are*?

❏ Do the verbs agree with their subjects?

❏ Do you format the paragraph correctly?

FLYING HIGH AND LOW

OVERVIEW

Theme: Famous people

Prewriting: Making a timeline

Organizing: Writing an autobiographical story

Revising: Using time order words
                Using the simple past

Editing: Punctuating time order words

Assignment

◆ Write a paragraph.

◆ Describe a trip you remember because it was very good (or very bad).

---

1 PREWRITING

MAKING A TIMELINE

 First, complete Unit 6, Sections 1–4, in the Student Book. Then, begin this section.

Making a timeline can help you remember your experiences. You can put the events in time order.

1 *Make a list of trips you remember. Think about trips you took to see family, to go on vacation, for business, or for school. They can be trips you enjoyed or trips you didn't enjoy. Look at the example on page 36.*

Example

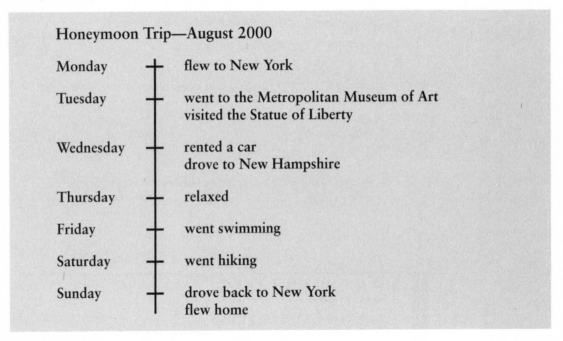

Trips
○ beach
| Grandmother's house
New York
○ honeymoon
London

2 *Choose one memorable trip from your list to write about. Then, look at the timeline of a honeymoon trip in August 2000.*

Honeymoon Trip—August 2000

Monday	flew to New York
Tuesday	went to the Metropolitan Museum of Art visited the Statue of Liberty
Wednesday	rented a car drove to New Hampshire
Thursday	relaxed
Friday	went swimming
Saturday	went hiking
Sunday	drove back to New York flew home

3 *Make a timeline of your trip on a separate piece of paper.*

ORGANIZING
WRITING AN AUTOBIOGRAPHICAL STORY

An autobiographical story is a story about the writer. The writer tells the story in time order starting with the first event and ending with the last event.

1 *Look back at the timeline in Prewriting, Exercise 2, on page 36. The paragraph below is about the honeymoon trip. The sentences are not in order. Put the sentences in order. Number the sentences from 1 to 8. The first one is done for you.*

_____ Then, we drove back to New York City on Sunday morning.

_____ Finally, we flew home on Sunday night. _____ It was a great honeymoon.

_1_ My husband and I had a wonderful honeymoon trip four years ago.

_____ On Wednesday, we rented a car and drove to New Hampshire. _____ We went swimming and hiking, and we relaxed. _____ The next day, we went to the Metropolitan Museum of Art and the Statue of Liberty. _____ First, we flew to New York City on Monday.

2 *Look at the timeline and complete the paragraph below. Put a check (✓) next to the topic sentence.*

Vacation in Florida

Monday	┼	almost missed our plane lost our luggage arrived in Florida
Tuesday	┼	went shopping for new clothes
Wednesday	┼	rained
Thursday	┼	rained
Friday	┼	stopped raining went to the beach
Saturday	┼	went home

Five years ago, my friend and I had a terrible vacation in Florida. Everything went wrong. First, we _____. Then, we _____. We arrived in Florida with no clothes, so we _____. Next, it _____ for two days. Finally, it stopped raining, and we _____. Then, we _____ the next day. It was a terrible vacation.

❸ *Look at your timeline of a memorable trip from Prewriting, Exercise 3, on page 36. Write a topic sentence for your paragraph. Tell where you went and why you remember the trip.*

Writing the First Draft

Now you are ready to write your first draft.

◆ Write a paragraph about a memorable trip.

◆ Begin with the topic sentence from Exercise 3, above.

◆ Put the events in time order.

Don't worry about grammar. Just try to make your ideas clear.

PEER REVIEW

Work with a partner. Read your partner's first draft. Answer the questions below. Then discuss your answers with your partner.

◆ Where did the writer go?

◆ Why was the trip memorable?

◆ Ask your partner one question about the trip.

REVISING

A. USING TIME ORDER WORDS

 First, complete Unit 6, Section 6B, in the Student Book. Then, begin this section.

Time order words show the order of events. Time order words help your reader understand your story. Time order words usually come at the beginning of a sentence.

I went hiking with my brother last week.

First, we put on our new hiking shoes.

Then, we put our food and water on our backs.

Next, my brother gave me his food because his backpack was too heavy.

Later, he gave me his water because his backpack was still too heavy.

Finally, we got to the top of the mountain.

Hiking is fun, but not with my brother!

Other time words show when an event happened or for how long:

Last year, I went to New York. *(last week, last month, yesterday)*

We left **the next day.** *(the next week, the next month, the next year)*

I went to New York **two years ago.** *(two months ago, two weeks ago, two days ago)*

We went to Florida **for a week.** *(for an hour, for a month, for a year)*

On Wednesday, we drove to New Hampshire. *(on Tuesday, on Friday, on Saturday)*

1 *Look back at the paragraph about the trip to Florida in Organizing, Exercise 2, on page 37. Underline the time order words or other time words.*

2 *Look at the timeline below. Complete the paragraph about the timeline with the time order words or other time words from the box. Capitalize the words if you need to. The first one is done for you.*

1998 Trip to Macchu Picchu

Monday — went from Lima to Cuzco

Tuesday
10:00 a.m.–4:00 p.m. — went up to Macchu Picchu
walked around
took pictures

Wednesday — went back to Lima

| the next day | ~~on Monday~~ | for about six hours | finally |

In 1998, my sister and I had a wonderful visit to Macchu Picchu, the old Inca city in Peru. ___On Monday___ (1.), we went from Lima to Cuzco. _____ (2.), we went up the mountain to Macchu Picchu. We walked around and took pictures _____ (3.). We were really tired, but it was very interesting. We learned about the Incan people. _____ (4.), we went back to Lima on Wednesday. We want to visit again soon.

❸ *Look at the first draft of your paragraph. Underline the time order words. Is the order of events clear? Add or change time order words to make your paragraph clear.*

B. USING THE SIMPLE PAST

 First, complete Unit 6, Section 6A, in the Student Book. Then, begin this section.

❶ *Complete the paragraph with the simple past tense of each verb. Six of the verbs are irregular. The first one is done for you.*

> In 1984, my family _____**went**_____ to the seashore. It
>   1. go
>
> _____ my first trip to the ocean. However, we _____
>   2. be   3. have
>
> a terrible trip. First, it _____ six hours to get there. Traffic was
>   4. take
>
> bad. Finally, we _____ at the seashore, but the nice hotel
>   5. arrive
>
> _____ any rooms. So we had to stay in a small, dirty hotel next
>   6. not have
>
> to the highway. We _____ to the beach the next day. We
>   7. go
>
> _____ for a few hours. Then, I cut my foot on some glass. It
>   8. stay
>
> hurt a lot and I cried. We _____ the next day.
>   9. leave

❷ *Look at the first draft of your paragraph. Underline all the simple past tense verbs. Make sure you use the correct form of each simple past tense verb.*

Writing the Second Draft

Now you are ready to write your second draft. Look at your first draft. Be sure you:

◆ use time order words to make the order of events clear.

◆ use the correct form of simple past tense verbs.

Now, rewrite your first draft.

EDITING

PUNCTUATING TIME ORDER WORDS

Use a comma after a time order word that is at the beginning of a sentence.

First,
Then,
Last year,   I went to the beach.
The next day,
On Saturday,

❶ *Underline the time order words and other time words in the paragraph. Six commas are missing. Add the commas.*

> Last summer I visited my grandparents at the beach for two weeks. It was my first trip away from home by myself. I had a good time, but every day we did the same thing. First we ate breakfast on the porch outside and watched the ocean. Then we walked on the beach. The sand was very hot. Next we went swimming. Later we visited some of my grandparents' friends. Next summer I will visit my other grandparents in the mountains.

❷ *Look at your second draft. Underline the time order words. Make sure you use commas correctly.*

Preparing the Final Draft

Carefully edit your second draft. Use the checklist below. Then neatly write or type your paragraph with the corrections.

FINAL DRAFT CHECKLIST

❑ Do you write an autobiographical story about a memorable trip?

❑ Do you include a topic sentence?

❑ Do you write the events in the order they happened?

❑ Do you use time order words?

❑ Do you use the simple past tense correctly?

❑ Do you format the paragraph correctly?

❑ Do you punctuate time order words correctly?

ARE WE THERE YET?

OVERVIEW

Theme:	Driving problems
Prewriting:	Making a chart
Organizing:	Outlining
Revising:	Giving reasons Using comparative adjectives
Editing:	Correcting run-on sentences

Assignment

◆ Write a paragraph.

◆ Describe the best way for you to get to school or work.

◆ Explain why this way is better than another way.

PREWRITING

MAKING A CHART

 First, complete Unit 7, Sections 1–4, in the Student Book. Then, begin this section.

Making a chart can help you compare two things. For example, you can list good things (advantages) and bad things (disadvantages).

❶ *Read the following chart. It shows advantages and disadvantages for two different ways to get to work.*

Ways to Get to Work	Advantages	Disadvantages

DRIVING	don't get wet when it rains	slower
		stressful
		    —traffic is bad
		    —hard to find parking
		don't get exercise

WALKING	get exercise not stressful faster don't have to park	get wet when it rains

2 *Choose two ways that you can get to school or work (for example, driving; taking the bus, train, or subway; walking; or riding a bicycle). Make a chart on a separate piece of paper. List the advantages and disadvantages of both ways. Use the questions below to help you. Think of your own ideas.*

- Is it more or less convenient? (How easy is it?)

- Is it more or less comfortable?

- Is it faster or slower?

- Is it expensive or cheap?

- Is there a lot of traffic?

- Does it pollute[1] the air?

3 *Look at your chart. Compare the advantages and disadvantages of both ways. Then, choose the best way for you to get to work or school.*

ORGANIZING

OUTLINING

Outlining helps you organize your ideas. It shows your main idea and the reasons and explanations that support it.

---

[1] *pollute:* to make dirty

1 *Read the paragraph.*

> Walking to work is better than driving to work. One reason is that walking to my job is usually faster than driving. This is because the traffic is bad, and it moves slowly. Another reason is that walking is less stressful than driving. I can relax when I walk. I get upset when there is a lot of traffic. The most important reason is that I get exercise when I walk. My office is one mile from my house. I don't get any exercise when I drive. For all these reasons, walking to work is better than driving.

2 *Work with a partner. Complete the outline about the paragraph above. Add the reasons.*

Reasons

Faster to walk
Less stressful than driving
Get more exercise

Outline

Main idea: Walking is better than driving.

Reason 1: _____

　Explanation: Traffic moves slowly.

Reason 2: _____

　Explanation: There is a lot of traffic. I don't relax.

Reason 3: _____

　Explanation: I walk one mile each way.

3 *Write an outline of your paragraph. Use ideas from the chart you made in Prewriting, Exercise 2, on page 43.*

Writing the First Draft

Now you are ready to write your first draft.

◆　Write a topic sentence. Tell which way is better for you to get to work or school.

◆　Give three reasons why one way is better than the other.

◆　Explain your reasons.

Don't worry about grammar. Just try to make your ideas clear.

PEER REVIEW

Work with a partner. Read your partner's first draft. Answer the questions below. Then discuss your answers with your partner.

- ◆ What is the best way for the writer to get to school or work?

- ◆ What is one reason the writer gives?

- ◆ What is one explanation for that reason?

---

3 REVISING

A. GIVING REASONS

Use transition words or phrases to introduce each reason in your paragraph. Some transition words and phrases show that your reasons are all equally important:

First,
In addition, } driving is more comfortable than taking the train.
Finally,

One reason is that
Another reason is that } driving is more comfortable than taking the train.
A third/final reason is that

Other transition phrases show that one or two reasons are more important.

The most important reason is that
Another (important) reason is that } driving is more comfortable than taking the train.
A final reason is that

1 *Read the paragraph in Organizing, Exercise 1, on page 44. Underline the transition words that introduce reasons. Then answer the question below.*

Is any reason more important than the others? If so, which one? Write it below.

_____

_____

2 *Read the list of reasons why flying is better than driving. Then work with a partner. Decide which are the three best reasons. Check (✔) them.*

Reasons

❏ Flying is faster. Driving can take all day.

❏ Flying is more comfortable. You can get up and walk around.

❏ Flight attendants bring you food and drinks. You don't have to stop at a restaurant.

❏ Airplanes are more fun. For example, on many planes you can use the Internet and watch movies.

❏ You can sleep on an airplane, so you are not tired when you get to the place you are going.

3 *Work with a partner. Complete the paragraph with the three best reasons you chose in, Exercise 2. Use transition words or phrases to introduce each reason. Is one reason more important than the others? If so, use transition words to show it.*

> **I like flying better than driving.** _____
>
> _____
>
> _____
>
> _____
>
> _____
>
> _____
>
> **For all these reasons, flying is better than driving.**

B. USING COMPARATIVE ADJECTIVES

 First, complete Unit 7, Section 6A, in the Student Book. Then, begin this section.

1 *Complete the sentences in the list that follows. Use comparative adjectives. The first one is done for you.*

1. Walking is ___**better than**___ driving. *(good)*

2. Walking to work is _____ driving. *(healthy)*

3. Walking is _____ driving. *(slow)*

4. Driving a car is _____ walking. *(expensive)*

5. Driving is _____ walking. *(enjoyable)*

6. Driving is _____ walking. *(difficult)*

2 *Read the paragraph. The comparative adjectives are underlined. There are four errors. Correct the errors. The first one is done for you.*

> **better**
> Traveling by airplane is ~~more good~~ than taking the train. The first reason is that an airplane is much <u>faster</u> a train. For example, it only takes one hour to fly from Boston to Washington, D.C. The train takes almost seven hours. Another reason is that getting to the airport is <u>easier than</u> getting to the train station. The airport is <u>more closer</u> to my house. A final reason is airplanes are <u>comfortabler than</u> trains. There is more room and the seats are <u>bigger</u>. For all these reasons, I prefer to travel by airplane.

3 *Look at the first draft of your paragraph. Do you use comparative adjectives? If not, add one or two comparative adjectives to your paragraph.*

Writing the Second Draft

Now you are ready to write your second draft. Look at your first draft. Be sure you:

- use transition words or phrases to introduce the reasons.
- use comparative adjectives correctly.

Now, rewrite your first draft.

EDITING

CORRECTING RUN-ON SENTENCES

A run-on sentence is two sentences put together with no punctuation between them. To correct run-on sentences, add a period between the two sentences. Make sure each of the sentences has a subject and a verb. See the examples following on page 48.

Incorrect: Traveling by train takes longer it takes almost seven hours.

Correct: Traveling by train takes longer. It takes almost seven hours.

1 *Read the run-on sentences. Then, correct them. Rewrite them on the lines. The first one is done for you.*

1. Walking to work is healthier than driving you get more exercise.

   <u>**Walking to work is healthier than driving. You get more exercise.**</u>

2. I enjoy walking to work because I have time to relax I don't worry about the traffic.

   _____

3. Traveling by train is not comfortable sometimes there is no place to sit down.

   _____

4. I like flying better than taking the train I like to look out the window and see the land below us.

   _____

2 *Look at your second draft. Be sure you correct any run-on sentences.*

Preparing the Final Draft

Carefully edit your second draft. Use the checklist below. Then neatly write or type your paragraph with the corrections.

FINAL DRAFT CHECKLIST

❏ Do you include a topic sentence?

❏ Do you tell what the best way for you to get to school or work is?

❏ Do you give three reasons?

❏ Do you explain your reasons?

❏ Do you use comparative adjectives?

❏ Do you format the paragraph correctly?

❏ Do you punctuate the sentences correctly?

FULL HOUSE

OVERVIEW

Theme:	Family
Prewriting:	Clustering
Organizing:	Writing concluding sentences
Revising:	Giving reasons with *because*
	Making predictions with *Be going to*
Editing:	Correcting incomplete sentences

Assignment

◆ Write a paragraph.

◆ Describe a person in your family.

◆ Explain why the person is special.

---

1 PREWRITING

CLUSTERING

 First, complete Unit 8, Sections 1–4, in the Student Book. Then, begin this section.

Clustering helps you organize your ideas and see how they are connected. In a cluster diagram, the main idea is in a large circle in the middle of the page. New ideas are in smaller circles and connected to the main idea with lines.

1 *Look at the cluster diagram on page 50. It tells about Edie, the writer's sister. For example, it shows that Edie is adventurous and smart. Some ideas are missing. Write the ideas given above the cluster diagram in the correct circles in the diagram.*

Europe	paints	French	math	CREATIVE

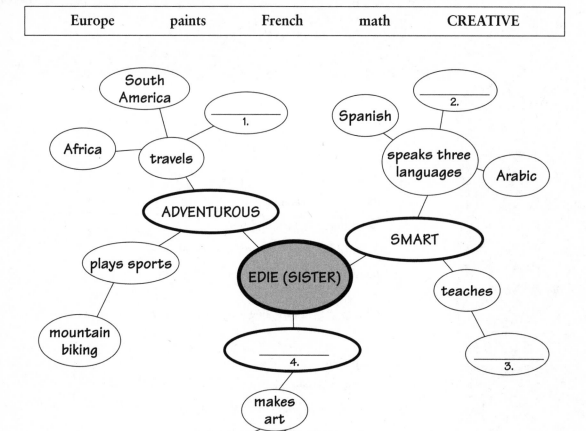

2 *Work with a partner. Look at the cluster diagram above. Answer the questions about Edie.*

1. Why is Edie smart? Give two reasons.

   _____

   _____

2. Why is Edie adventurous? Give two reasons.

   _____

   _____

3. Why is Edie creative? Give one reason.

   _____

3 *Choose a family member to write about. Make a cluster diagram about your family member. On a separate piece of paper:*

♦ Write the person's name in a circle in the middle.

♦ Add adjectives in circles around the name. Connect the adjectives to the name with lines.

♦ Write reasons or examples next to the adjectives. Connect them to the adjectives with lines.

♦ Use the cluster diagram on page 50 to help you.

ORGANIZING
WRITING CONCLUDING SENTENCES

A concluding sentence is the last sentence in a paragraph. A concluding sentence usually says the main idea again. Sometimes it adds a new idea or an opinion.

1 *Read the paragraph. Then read the three concluding sentences. Work with a partner and answer the questions below.*

> I admire my sister Edie. She is an adventurous person. She likes to see new places and meet new people. Last year, she traveled to South America and Africa. Edie is also very smart. She teaches math at a university. She also likes to learn new languages. She speaks French, Spanish, and some Arabic. In addition, Edie is an artist. She paints and draws. _____
>
> _____

Concluding Sentences

    a. For all these reasons, I admire my sister.

    b. I think my sister is a wonderful person.

    c. For all these reasons, I think my sister will be successful in life.

1. Which concluding sentence tells the main idea of the paragraph again? _____

2. Which concluding sentence gives an opinion? _____

3. Which concluding sentence adds a new idea? _____

4. Which concluding sentence do you think is the best? Tell your partner why.

2 *The concluding sentence supports the topic sentence. Match each topic sentence with its concluding sentence. Write the letter of the concluding sentence next to the topic sentence.*

Topic Sentences	Concluding Sentences
_____ 1. My father has an interesting job.	**a.** I want to be like my father when I have children.
_____ 2. My father has worked hard to be a success.	**b.** I admire my father for working so hard.
_____ 3. My father takes good care of our family.	**c.** I would like to have a job like my father's.

3 *Look at the cluster diagram you made in Prewriting, Exercise 3, on page 51. Write a topic sentence for your paragraph.*

Writing the First Draft

Now you are ready to write your first draft.

◆ Write a paragraph about a special person in your family. Explain why that person is special.

◆ Include a topic sentence.

◆ Use adjectives. Give reasons or examples for each adjective.

◆ Include a concluding sentence.

Don't worry about grammar. Just try to make your ideas clear.

PEER REVIEW

Work with a partner. Read your partner's first draft. Answer the questions below. Then, discuss your answers with a partner.

◆ Who is the paragraph about?

◆ Is there a clear topic sentence and concluding sentence?

◆ Does the writer use adjectives? What are they?

◆ Ask your partner one question about the person.

REVISING

A. GIVING REASONS WITH *Because*

  First, complete Unit 8, Section 6B, in the Student Book. Then, begin this section.

You can use *because* to introduce a reason. *Because* answers the question "Why?"

❶ *Read the paragraph. Two of the underlined sentence pairs can be combined with* because. *One pair cannot be combined. Rewrite the sentences that can be combined on a separate piece of paper. Use* because.

> My sister Edie is a very special person. (<u>I don't see her very often. She lives in California.</u>) Edie is an adventurous person. Last year, she traveled to South America and Africa. She likes to see new places and meet new people. Edie is also very smart. She teaches math. (<u>She also likes to learn new languages. She can speak French, Spanish, and some Arabic.</u>) In addition, she is also an artist. I have several of her paintings in my house. (<u>My sister is going to be successful. She is very smart.</u>) For all these reasons, I admire my sister.

❷ *Look at the first draft of your paragraph. Do you give reasons with* because? *Find at least two places where you can use* because. *Add new information to your paragraph if you need to.*

B. MAKING PREDICTIONS WITH *Be going to*

  First, complete Unit 8, Section 6A, in the Student Book. Then, begin this section.

Use *be going to* to make predictions about the future.

❶ *Use the words to make sentences with* be going to. *The first one is done for you.*

1. My sister / be successful   <u>My sister is going to be successful.</u>

2. She / visit France again.   _____

3. My father / get a new job.   _____

4. I / see my uncle soon.   _____

5. My parents / retire next year.   _____

2 *The sentences below are not correct. Correct the errors. The first one is done for you.*

1. My brother is going ^{to} teach at a university.

2. He ∧ not going to work in a business.

3. My sister and her boyfriend is going to get married soon.

4. They are go to have a nice honeymoon.

5. My sister is going to having an art show.

3 *Look at the first draft of your paragraph. Do you make any predictions with* be going to? *If not, add one prediction. Make sure you use* be going to *correctly.*

Writing the Second Draft

Now you are ready to write your second draft. Look at your first draft. Be sure you:

◆ give reasons with *because*.

◆ use *be going to* to make predictions about the future.

EDITING

CORRECTING INCOMPLETE SENTENCES

In Unit 1, you learned that every sentence must have a subject and a verb.

Look at the incorrect and correct sentences below.

Incorrect:	My sister is adventurous. <u>Travels around the world.</u>
Correct:	My sister is adventurous. <u>She</u> travels around the world. *(Correction: Add a subject.)*
Incorrect:	My sister is going to be successful. <u>Because she is very smart.</u>
Correct:	My sister is going to be successful because she is very smart. *(Correction: Combine the incomplete and complete sentence with* because.*)*

1 *Underline the incorrect sentences. Then write the correct sentence on the line. The first one is done for you.*

1. She likes mathematics. <u>Because it is interesting.</u>

   <u>She likes mathematics because it is interesting.</u>

2. My sister is an artist. Paints pictures and draws.

   _____

3. She likes to travel. Because she is very adventurous.

   _____

4. Speaks French. She studied it in high school.

   _____

5. My sister has a PhD. Teaches at the university.

   _____

6. She works very hard. Because she enjoys her work.

   _____

2 *Look at your second draft. Underline any sentences with errors. Then correct them.*

Preparing the Final Draft

Carefully edit your second draft. Use the checklist below. Then neatly write or type your paragraph with the corrections.

FINAL DRAFT CHECKLIST

❑ Is your paragraph about a special person in your family?

❑ Does it have a topic sentence and concluding sentence?

❑ Does it have descriptive words that tell why the person is special?

❑ Do you include reasons with *because*?

❑ Do you include predictions with *be going to*?

❑ Do you format the paragraph correctly?

❑ Are the sentences correct?

IT'S YOUR LUCKY DAY!

OVERVIEW

Theme: Money

Prewriting: Choosing a prewriting technique

Organizing: Expressing an opinion

Revising: Supporting an opinion
Using *should*

Editing: Editing a paragraph

Assignment

◆ Write a paragraph.

◆ Give your opinion: "What do you think lottery winners should do with their money?"

◆ Explain your opinion. Try to persuade (convince) the reader to agree with you.

1 PREWRITING

CHOOSING A PREWRITING TECHNIQUE

 First, complete Unit 9, Sections 1–4, in the Student Book. Then, begin this section.

1 *What do you think lottery winners should do with their money? Check (✓) agree or disagree. Write your own idea on the line. Then compare your answers with the class.*

Lottery winners should . . .	Agree	Disagree
a. keep all the money for themselves.	❏	❏
b. share the money with their families.	❏	❏
c. share the money with their friends.	❏	❏
d. give some money to charities (groups that help other people).	❏	❏
e. Your idea: _____		

2 *You learned about eight prewriting techniques in this book. You can use all these techniques to get ideas to write. Work with a partner. Look at the prewriting techniques. Think about each technique. Which techniques are helpful for this assignment? Which techniques are not?*

- Interviewing (Unit 1, page 1)
- Finding information in a reading (Unit 2, page 7)
- Questioning yourself (Unit 3, page 13)
- Listing (Unit 4, page 20)
- Drawing a picture (Unit 5, page 28)
- Making a timeline (Unit 6, page 35)
- Making a chart (Unit 7, page 43)
- Clustering (Unit 8, page 49)

3 *What is your opinion:* What should lottery winners do with their money? *Use two prewriting techniques from the list above. Use them both to get ideas for your paragraph. Think of reasons and examples to support your opinion. Write them on a separate piece of paper.*

4 *Work in a small group. Discuss these questions.*

- Which prewriting techniques did you use?
- Which one was more helpful? Why?

ORGANIZING

EXPRESSING AN OPINION

There are three things you need to do when you are expressing your opinion in writing.

1. Express your opinion in your topic sentence.

2. Give reasons to support your opinion.

3. Use examples to explain your reasons.

Here are some ways to express an opinion:

In my opinion, . . .	I believe (that) . . .
I don't believe (that) . . .	I don't think (that) . . .
I feel (that) . . .	I don't feel (that) . . .
I think (that) . . .	

❶ *Read the paragraph. Then complete the tasks below.*

> In my opinion, lottery winners should give some of their money to charity. The first reason is that most lottery winners win a lot of money. For example, a man recently won over 15 million dollars in the Big Game lottery. I don't think he should spend 15 million dollars. He should give some of the money to charity, and he should keep some for himself. Another reason is that giving money to charity makes people feel good. For example, I gave $5 to the children's hospital. I felt really good because I was helping sick children. For these reasons, I believe that lottery winners should give away some of their money.

a. Circle the words that express an opinion. The first one is done for you.

b. Underline the topic sentence.

c. Underline the concluding sentence.

d. Circle the words that introduce a reason.

e. Circle the words that introduce an example.

❷ *Use your ideas from Prewriting, Exercise 3, on page 57 to complete the outline of your paragraph.*

Main idea: _____

   Reason 1: _____

      Example: _____

   Reason 2: _____

      Example: _____

Concluding sentence: _____

Writing the First Draft

Now you are ready to write your first draft.

- Express your opinion about what lottery winners should do with their money.

- Write a topic sentence. Begin the sentence "I think lottery winners should . . . ."

- Give two reasons to support your opinion.

- Use examples to explain your reasons.

- Write a concluding sentence that tells your main idea again, adds new information, or gives an opinion.

Don't worry about grammar. Just try to make your ideas clear.

PEER REVIEW

Work with a partner. Read your partner's first draft. Answer the questions below. Then discuss your answers with your partner.

- What does the writer think lottery winners should do with their money?

- What reasons and examples does the writer give to support his or her opinion?

---

3 REVISING

A. SUPPORTING AN OPINION

When you express your opinion, you want your reader to agree with you. You can give specific examples to support your opinion.

A **specific example** is something you know from your experience or the experience of someone else. You can use a general statement to introduce a specific example:

> Winning the lottery can cause problems. (**general statement**) One example is the story of Jeffrey Johnson. He won the lottery. Then, he argued with his mother about the money. Now, they don't speak to each other. (**specific example**)

① *Read the pairs of statements. Match the general statements with the specific examples. The first one is done for you.*

General Statements

_b_ 1. Many rich people are unhappy.

_____ 2. Playing the lottery is a waste of money.

_____ 3. Some people win a lot of money in the lottery.

_____ 4. It's fun to play the lottery.

Specific Examples

a. Jeffrey Johnson won 2.5 million dollars.

b. Christina Onassis was the richest woman in the world. However, she was never happy. She never found true love.

c. I buy lottery tickets with my lucky numbers. I never win, but I enjoy playing.

d. My uncle spends $10 a week on lottery tickets, but he never wins.

② *Work with a partner. Look back at the paragraph in Organizing, Exercise 1, on page 58. Then answer the questions.*

1. What are two specific examples?

_____

_____

2. What two general statements introduce the examples?

_____

_____

③ *Look at the first draft of your paragraph. Do you use general statements to introduce specific examples? If necessary, add general statements or specific examples to your paragraph.*

B. USING *Should*

 First, complete Unit 9, Section 6A, in the Student Book. Then, begin this exercise.

① *What should lottery winners do? Complete the sentences with* should *or* shouldn't. *The first one is done for you.*

1. Lottery winners ___should___ split the money with their family.

2. Lottery winners _____ put the money in a bank.

3. Lottery winners _____ buy a new house.

4. Lottery winners _____ go on TV.

5. Lottery winners _____ give some of the money to poor people.

6. Lottery winners _____ stop talking to their friends.

2 *The sentences below are not correct. Underline the errors. Then write the correct sentence on the line. The first one is done for you.*

1. You <u>should to play</u> the lottery. It's fun!

   You should play the lottery. It's fun!

2. My parents shouldn't spending all their money on lottery tickets.

   _____

3. Jeffrey should not fights with his parents.

   _____

4. Families should sharing their lottery money.

   _____

5. Jeffrey shoulds not be greedy.

   _____

6. He should his money.

   _____

3 *Look at the first draft of your paragraph. Do you use* should? *If not, add a sentence with* should. *Make sure you use* should *correctly.*

Writing the Second Draft

Now you are ready to write your second draft. Look at your first draft. Be sure you:

* use general statements and specific examples.

* use *should correctly.*

Now, rewrite your first draft.

EDITING

EDITING A PARAGRAPH

In this book, you learned to:

◆ write sentences correctly. (Unit 1, page 6)

◆ use commas correctly. (Unit 2, page 11, and Unit 6, page 41)

◆ format a paragraph correctly. (Unit 3, page 18)

◆ correct subject-verb agreement. (Unit 5, page 33)

◆ correct run-on sentences. (Unit 7, page 47)

◆ correct incomplete sentences. (Unit 8, page 54)

❶ *Read the sentences. Each sentence has one type of error. Underline the errors. Write the correct sentence on the line. The first one is done for you.*

1. <u>First</u> I think that most lottery winners need the money.

   <u>First, I think that most lottery winners need the money.</u>

2. i don't feel that lottery winners should give their money to charity

   _____

3. For example, I play the lottery every day. Because I need money for my family.

   _____

4. I want to buy a new house my children need money for their education.

   _____

5. In addition, my father need money for medical care. If I win, I won't give any money to charity.

   _____

❷ *Look at your second draft. Correct the errors in your paragraph.*

Preparing the Final Draft

Carefully edit your second draft. Use the following checklist. Then neatly write or type your paragraph with the corrections.

FINAL DRAFT CHECKLIST

❑ Do you express your opinion?

❑ Do you have a topic sentence and a concluding sentence?

❑ Do you include reasons and specific examples?

❑ Do you use *should* correctly?

❑ Do you format the paragraph correctly?

❑ Is the punctuation correct?

Answer Key

Note: For exercises where no answers are given, answers will vary.

UNIT 1 ◆
THE FRIENDSHIP PAGE

1. PREWRITING
(pages 1–2)

1
2. Where are you from?
3. How old are you?
4. What is your job?
5. What are your hobbies or interests?
6. Who is your best friend?
7. Where is he (or she) from?
8. How old is he (or she)?
9. What is his (or her) job?
10. What are his (or her) hobbies or interests?

2. ORGANIZING
(page 3)

3 Description 1

    My classmate's name is Fernando. He is from Spain. He is 21 years old. He is a student in Chicago. Fernando is friendly. He likes going to parties. Fernando's best friend is Ricardo. He is from Spain. He is 20 years old. He is a student in Madrid. Ricardo is friendly and athletic. He likes going to parties and playing sports. (There are no sentences about both Fernando and Ricardo).

Description 2

    My classmate's name is Fernando. His best friend is Ricardo. Fernando is from Spain. He is 21 years old. Ricardo is also from Spain. He is 20 years old. Fernando is a student in Chicago. Ricardo is a student in Madrid. Fernando and Ricardo are both friendly. They like going to parties. Ricardo also likes playing sports.

3. REVISING
A. (page 4)

1 *Put a star next to the following sentences:*
Fernando is friendly.
Ricardo is friendly and athletic.

2 2. i 3. f 4. d 5. g 6. a 7. e 8. c
9. h 10. j

3 Answers will vary.

B. (page 5)

1 2. is 3. is 4. is 5. is 6. is 7. are
8. are

2 *Put a check next to sentences 3 and 6.*

4. EDITING
(page 6)

1 (1) ~~my~~ ^Mclassmate's name is Bernard. (2) He is 24 years old. (3) He is from Senegal. (4) ~~Likes~~ ^{He likes} playing soccer and going out dancing.
(5) Bernard's friend ^{is}Alexandre. (6) He is from France. (7) He ^{is}intelligent and shy. (8) ~~he~~ ^{He} likes going to the beach and reading.

UNIT 2 ◆
ART FOR EVERYONE

1. PREWRITING
(pages 7–8)

1
2. He died in 1990.
3. He was arrested in 1981 for drawing in the subway.
4. He was an art student at the School for Visual Arts from 1978 to 1979.
5. His first drawings were graffiti. They were in the subway of New York City.
6. His first important art show was at the Tony Shafrazi Gallery in New York City.

2. ORGANIZING
(page 8)

❶ a. 2   b. 6   c. 7   d. 5   e. 1   f. 3   g. 4

3. REVISING
A. (page 10)

❶ 2. 1942   3. 1947   4. 1948   5. 1951

❷   Rauschenberg was born in Port Arthur, Texas, in 1925. (In 1942,) he was a student at the University of Texas. He was a student and studied art at the Kansas City Art Institute from <u>1947 to 1948.</u> His first important show was in New York City <u>in 1951.</u> Today, people call him the "Father of Pop Art."

B. (page 11)

❶ 2. were   3. was   4. was   5. was   6. was
7. was   8. wasn't

4. EDITING
(page 12)

❶   Roy Lichtenstein was born in New York in 1923. From 1946 to 1949**,** he was an art student at Ohio State University in Columbus**,** Ohio. His first art show was in 1951. He made paintings, drawings, and sculptures. Some of his paintings were very popular. For example**,** his most popular paintings were cartoons. His art is in museums all over the world**,** and he is still very famous. Lichtenstein died in 1997.

UNIT 3 ◆
WHAT'S IT WORTH TO YOU?

2. ORGANIZING
(pages 14–15)

❶ *Topic sentence:* One of my special possessions is my collection of family photographs.

❷ *Topic sentence:* b

3. REVISING
A. (page 16)

❷   <u>My bicycle is a very special possession.</u> My bike is not worth a lot of money. It is old, but it is in good condition. I ride my bike everyday. I ride it to school, to the store, and to visit my friends. ~~I also know how to drive a car.~~ I can go wherever I want because I have a bike.

B. (page 17)

❶ 2. own   3. includes   4. don't know
5. enjoy   6. want

❷   My most special possession ~~are~~ *is* my favorite cookbook. My favorite cookbook ~~are~~ *is* from my grandmother. It ~~have~~ *has* recipes that she made for me when I was a child. I also ~~having~~ *have* cookbooks from all over the world. I ~~likes~~ *like* to taste new kinds of food. My cookbook collection ~~give~~ *gives* me a lot of ideas for new recipes.

4. EDITING
(page 18)

❶

Did the writer . . .	Paragraph 1	Paragraph 2
◆ indent the first line of the paragraph?	No	Yes
◆ write between the left and right margins?	No	Yes
◆ begin new sentences on the same line?	No	Yes

UNIT 4 ◆
STRENGTH IN NUMBERS

2. ORGANIZING
(page 23)

❷ 1. Maude Moran is a high school art teacher.
2. She is writing about the Neighborhood Art Center.
3. She supports it because it has art classes for children and adults and it supports local artists.

3. REVISING
A. (pages 24–25)

Underline the following sentences:

The Urban Angels help teenagers avoid problems such as drugs, crimes, and gangs.
For example, they paint over graffiti at neighborhood "paint-outs."

❷ 3. The Neighborhood Art Center has classes for all ages, such as children, college students, adults, and senior citizens.
4. The art classes are not expensive. For example, a drawing class costs only $15 per semester.
5. The Neighborhood Art Center supports local artists. For example, local artists teach classes at the Art Center.
6. The gift shop sells art by local artists, such as jewelry, paintings, and pottery.

B. (pages 25–26)

❶ 1. The Urban Angels help teenagers avoid problems. They want teenagers to stay in school.

2. Teenagers can take classes about social issues. They learn how to take care of themselves.

3. The Urban Angels help their city. They paint over graffiti at neighborhood "paint-outs." At park cleanups, they go to city parks and make them beautiful again.

❷ 2. They   3. their   4. it   5. them   6. It
7. They   8. They   9. them

4. EDITING
(page 27)

❶

Letter to the Editor

greeting   (March 18, 2003) date
(Dear Editor,)   message

   I am a student in New York City. I am writing about an organization called the Urban Angels. The Urban Angels help teenagers avoid problems such as drugs, crime, and gangs. They want teenagers to stay in school. The Urban Angels have activities after school and on weekends. In addition, the Urban Angels help the community. Teenagers can take classes about social issues. They learn how to take care of themselves and stop problems in the community. Finally, the Urban Angels help their city. For example, they paint over graffiti at neighborhood "paint-outs." At park cleanups, they go to city parks and make them beautiful again. For all these reasons, I think people should support the Urban Angels.

closing   (Sincerely,)
signature   *Maurice Roberts*

UNIT 5 ◆
GOING OUT OF BUSINESS

1. PREWRITING
(page 29)

❷ 1. The Big Salad is a restaurant.
2. It is on Main Street. It is near the post office, bank, and department store.

2. ORGANIZING
(pages 30–31)

❶ 1. The writer is describing a restaurant called The Big Salad.
2. It is on Main Street. It is next to the post office and across from the department store.
3. It sells salad and soup.
4. The atmosphere is bright and cheerful.
5. The writer likes the food and the atmosphere.

❷ fresh   tasty   bright   great
large   big   cheerful

❸ 2. big   3. comfortable   4. next to the window   5. friendly   6. near my house

3. REVISING

A. (page 32)

❶ 2. next to   3. between   4. around the corner from   5. across from   6. in front of   7. to the right of   8. in front of

B. (pages 32–33)

Underline the following sentences:

❶ There is a large salad bar.
There are also tasty soups, such as chicken noodle, clam chowder, and onion.
There are big windows in the front.

❷ 2. There is soft <u>music</u> playing. (non-count noun)
3. There is delicious <u>ice cream</u>. (non-count noun)
4. There are some <u>tables</u> outside. (plural count noun)
5. There is a <u>salad bar</u>. (singular count noun)
6. There is a comfortable <u>chair</u>. (singular count noun)

4. EDITING

(page 34)

❶ 2. like   3. is   4. sell   5. sells   6. is   7. are

UNIT 6 ◆
FLYING HIGH AND LOW

2. ORGANIZING

(page 37)

❶   _6_ Then, we drove back to New York City on Sunday morning. _7_ Finally, we flew home on Sunday night. _8_ It was a great honeymoon. _1_ My husband and I had a wonderful honeymoon trip four years ago.
_4_ On Wednesday, we rented a car and drove to New Hampshire. _5_ We went swimming and hiking, and we relaxed. _3_ The next day, we went to the Metropolitan Museum of Art and the Statue of Liberty. _2_ First, we flew to New York City on Monday.

❷   ✓ Five years ago, my friend and I had a terrible vacation in Florida. Everything went wrong. First, we <u>almost missed our plane.</u> Then, we <u>lost our luggage.</u> We arrived in Florida with no clothes, so we <u>went shopping for new clothes.</u> Next, it <u>rained</u> for two days. Finally, it stopped raining, and we <u>went to the beach.</u> Then, we <u>went home</u> the next day. It was a terrible vacation.

3. REVISING

A. (page 39)

❶ *Underline the following words:* Five years ago, First, Then, Next, Finally, Then, the next day

❷ 2. The next day   3. for about six hours   4. Finally

B. (page 40)

❶ 2. was   3. had   4. took   5. arrived   6. didn't have   7. went   8. stayed   9. left

4. EDITING

(page 41)

❶   <u>Last summer,</u> I visited my grandparents at the beach <u>for two weeks</u>. It was my first trip away from home by myself. I had a good time, but <u>every day</u> we did the same thing. <u>First,</u> we ate breakfast on the porch outside and watched the ocean. <u>Then,</u> we walked on the beach. The sand was very hot. <u>Next,</u> we went swimming. <u>Later,</u> we visited some of my grandparents' friends. <u>Next summer,</u> I will visit my other grandparents in the mountains.

UNIT 7 ◆
ARE WE THERE YET?

2. ORGANIZING

(page 44)

❷ *Reason 1:* Walking is usually faster than driving.
Reason 2: Walking is less stressful than driving.
Reason 3: I get exercise when I walk.

3. REVISING
A. (pages 45–46)

❶ *Underline the following words:* One reason is . . . , Another reason is . . . , The most important reason is . . .
"I get exercise when I walk" is more important than the other reasons.

❷ Answers will vary.

❸ Answers will vary.

B. (pages 46–47)

❶ 2. healthier than   3. slower than   4. more expensive than   5. more enjoyable than
6. more difficult than

❷   Traveling by airplane is ~~more good~~ *better* than taking the train. The first reason is that an airplane is much faster *than* a train. For example, it only takes one hour to fly from Boston to Washington, D.C. The train takes almost seven hours. Another reason is that getting to the airport is easier than getting to the train station. The airport is ~~more~~ closer to my house. A final reason is airplanes are ~~comfortabler~~ *more comfortable* than trains. There is more room and the seats are bigger. For all these reasons, I prefer to travel by airplane.

4. EDITING
(page 48)

❶ 2. I enjoy walking to work because I have time to relax. I don't worry about the traffic.
3. Traveling by train is not comfortable. Sometimes there is no place to sit down.
4. I like flying better than taking the train. I like to look out the window and see the land below us.

UNIT 8 ◆
FULL HOUSE

1. PREWRITING
(page 50)

❶ 1. Europe   2. French   3. math
4. CREATIVE   5. paints

❷ *Possible answers:*
1. She teaches math and speaks three languages.
2. She travels and rides a mountain bike.
3. She makes art.

2. ORGANIZING
(pages 51–52)

❶ *Concluding sentence:* Answers will vary.
1. a   2. b   3. c   4. Answers will vary.

❷ 1. c   2. b   3. a

3. REVISING
A. (page 53)

❶ 1. I don't see her very often because she lives in California.
2. She is going to be successful because she is very smart.

B. (pages 53–54)

❶ 2. She is going to visit France again.
3. My father is going to get a new job.
4. I am going to see my uncle soon.
5. My parents are going to retire next year.

❷ 2. He *is* not going to work in a business.
3. My sister and her boyfriend ~~is~~ *are* going to get married soon.
4. They are ~~go~~ *going* to have a nice honeymoon.
5. My sister is going to ~~having~~ *have* an art show.

4. EDITING
(pages 54–55)

❶ 2. My sister is an artist. She paints pictures and draws.

3. She likes to travel because she is very adventurous.

4. She speaks French. She studied it in high school.

5. My sister has a PhD. She teaches at the university.

6. She works very hard because she enjoys her work.

UNIT 9 ◆
IT'S YOUR LUCKY DAY

2. ORGANIZING
(pages 58–59)

❶ a. *Circle the words that express an opinion:* In my opinion, I don't think, I believe.

b. *Underline the topic sentence:* In my opinion, lottery winners should give some of their money to charity.

c. *Underline the concluding sentence:* For these reasons, I believe that lottery winners should give away some of their money.

d. *Circle the words that introduce a reason:* The first reason is, Another reason is

e. *Circle the words that introduce an example:* For example

3. REVISING
A. (page 60)

❶ 2. d   3. a   4. c

❷ 1. A man recently won over 15 million dollars in the Big Game lottery.

I gave $5 dollars to the children's hospital.

2. Most lottery winners win a lot of money.

Giving money to charity makes people feel good.

B. (pages 60–61)

❶ Answers will vary.

❷ 2. My parents shouldn't **spend** all their money on lottery tickets.

3. Jeffrey should not **fight** with his parents.

4. Families should **share** their lottery money.

5. Jeffrey **should** not be greedy.

6. (Suggested answer) He should **spend** his money.

4. EDITING
(page 62)

❶ 2. I don't feel that lottery winners should give their money to charity**.** (Incorrect capitalization and punctuation)

3. For example, I play the lottery every **day because** I need money for my family. (Incomplete sentence)

4. I want to buy a new house**. My** children need money for their education. (Run-on sentence)

5. In addition, my father **needs** money for medical care. If I win, I won't give any money to charity. (Subject-verb agreement)